Math Counts

Length

Children's Press®

An Imprint of Scholastic Inc.

About This Series

In keeping with the major goals of the National Council of Teachers of Mathematics, children will become mathematical problem solvers, learn to communicate mathematically, and learn to reason mathematically by using the series Math Counts.

Pattern, Shape, and *Size* may be investigated first—in any sequence.

Sorting, Counting, and *Numbers* may be used next, followed by *Time, Length, Weight,* and *Capacity.*

—Ramona G. Choos, Professor of Mathematics,
Senior Adviser to the Dean of Continuing Education, Chicago State University;
Sponsor for Chicago Elementary Teachers' Mathematics Club

Author's Note

Mathematics is a part of a child's world. It is not only interpreting numbers or mastering tricks of addition or multiplication. Mathematics is about ideas. These ideas have been developed to explain particular qualities such as size, weight, and height, as well as relationships and comparisons. Yet all too often the important part that an understanding of mathematics will play in a child's development is forgotten or ignored.

Most adults can solve simple mathematical tasks without the need for counters, beads, or fingers. Young children find such abstractions almost impossible to master. They need to see, talk, touch, and experiment.

The photographs and text in these books have been chosen to encourage talk about topics that are essentially mathematical. By talking, the young reader can explore some of the central concepts that support mathematics. It is on an understanding of these concepts that a student's future mastery of mathematics will be built.

—Henry Pluckrose

Math Counts

By Henry Pluckrose

Mathematics Consultant: Ramona G. Choos, Professor of Mathematics

Children's Press®

An Imprint of Scholastic Inc.

How long is the string in this ball?

How long is this truck? Sometimes we need to measure things to find out exactly how long they are.

We use the word *length* to describe the measurement of something from one end to the other. We talk about the length of a swimming pool,

the length of a race,

the length of a highway,

or a length of fabric.

You could measure the length
of a table by counting in hand spans,

but people's hands are not all the same size.

You could measure the length of a lawn by counting paces,

but people's paces are not all the same size.

If we want to measure exactly, we have to use a standard measure. Standard measures are the same everywhere. A surveyor measures the ground with a tape. The tape is divided into feet and inches or meters and centimeters.

It is important to be able to measure exactly. Architects draw detailed plans for builders to use. They have to make sure a building will fit on its space.

A tailor uses exact measurements. Short lengths are measured in inches or centimeters. Thirty-six inches make one yard. One hundred centimeters make one meter.

Scientists often study very small creatures. Tiny things are measured in fractions of an inch or in millimeters. Ten millimeters make one centimeter, about one-third of an inch.

Yards and inches are useful for measuring things that are not too long. In some countries, distances between places are measured in miles. One mile equals 1,760 yards.

PROSPECT PARK ZOO
3.7 MILES

BOROUGH HALL
2.7 MILES

GRACIE MANSION
11.4 MILES

CONEY ISLAND
11.4 MILES

PANAMA CANAL
2,218 MI

PEORIA, IL
932 MILES

MASIAKA 20 Km

KAMBIA 103 Km

KABALA 241 Km

BO 186 Km

In many other countries, a different standard measure is used to show distances between places. This sign shows distances in kilometers. One thousand meters make one kilometer. A mile is longer than a kilometer.

We also use feet and inches, or meters and centimeters, to measure height. The height of a person is measured from the soles of the feet to the top of the head. What is your height?

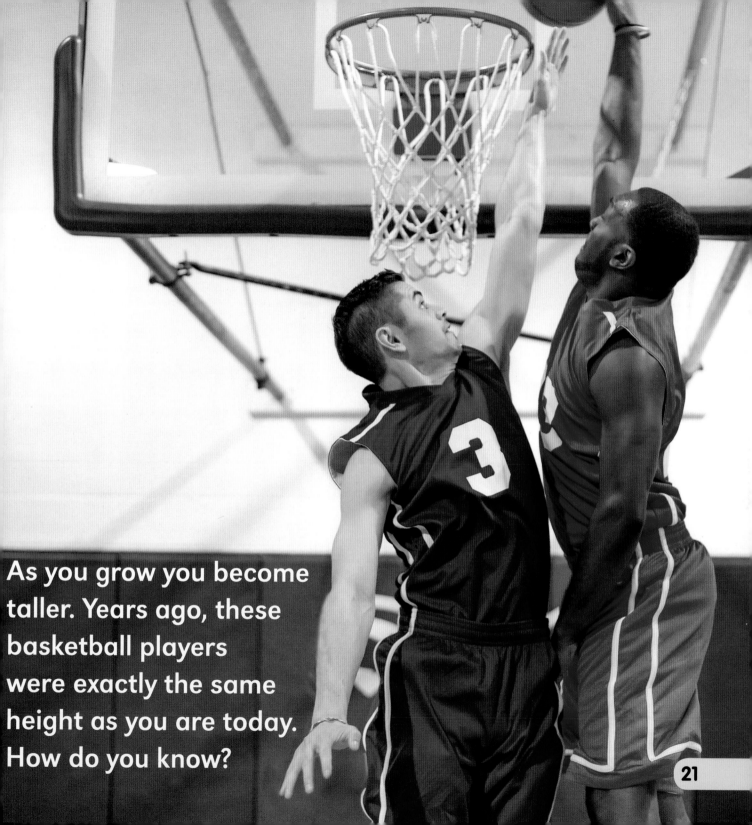

As you grow you become taller. Years ago, these basketball players were exactly the same height as you are today. How do you know?

21

We use the word *height* to describe many other things. The height of a building is measured from the ground to the very top.

The height of this cliff is measured from the level of the sea to the grassy land at the top.

Mountains also are measured from sea level. The peak, or top, of Mount Everest is 29,029 feet (8,848 meters) above sea level. Why is sea level used when giving the height of a mountain?

Aircraft pilots also measure the height at which their planes are flying.

We can describe the height of things around us by comparing them with the height of our own bodies. These plants have not grown very tall,

but they seem enormous
to an earthworm.

These trees are very tall.
Their topmost branches
are far above the ground.

When trees are cut down for timber, a lumberjack measures the length of each trunk, not its height.

What is the difference between length

and height?

Index

Reader's Guide

Visit this Scholastic Web site to download the Reader's Guide for this series:
www.factsfornow.scholastic.com Enter the keywords **Math Counts**

Library of Congress Cataloging-in-Publication Data

Names: Pluckrose, Henry, 1931- author. | Choos, Ramona G.
Title: Length/by Henry Pluckrose; mathematics consultant, Ramona G. Choos, Professor of Mathematics.
Other titles: Math counts.
Description: Updated edition. | New York, NY: Children's Press, an imprint of Scholastic Inc., 2019. | Series: Math counts | Includes index.
Identifiers: LCCN 2017061278| ISBN 9780531175088 (library binding) | ISBN 9780531135174 (pbk.)
Subjects: LCSH: Length measurement—Juvenile literature.
Classification: LCC QC102 .P58 2019 | DDC 530.8—dc23
LC record available at https://lccn.loc.gov/2017061278

Copyright © The Watts Publishing Group, 2018
Printed in Heshan, China 62

Scholastic Inc., 557 Broadway, New York, NY 10012.

1 2 3 4 5 6 7 8 9 10 R 28 27 26 25 24 23 22 21 20 19

Photos ©: cover top: Serjio74/iStockphoto; cover bottom: Roni Mocan; 1: Roni Mocan; 3: Roni Mocan; 4: fotyma/iStockphoto; 5: 3dmentat/iStockphoto; 6: Paolo Bona/Shutterstock; 7: Chris Smith/Popperfoto/Getty Images; 8: kbwills/iStockphoto; 9: picturegarden/Getty Images; 10-11: Jenna Addesso; 12-13: Joshua Moise; 14: Photographee.eu/Fotolia; 15: Education Images/Getty Images; 16: Maskot/Getty Images; 17: Serjio74/iStockphoto; 18: Randy Duchaine/Alamy Images; 19: lcoccia/iStockphoto; 20: Redlink Production/age fotostock; 21: FatCamera/iStockphoto; 22: EllenMoran/iStockphoto; 23: prestongeorge/iStockphoto; 24: Zzvet/iStockphoto; 25: Artpilot/iStockphoto; 26: Jupiterimages/Getty Images; 27: shaunl/iStockphoto; 28: Serjio74/iStockphoto; 29: Lena Ason/Alamy Images; 30: FangXiaNuo/iStockphoto; 31: Michael Dodge/Getty Images.